D1519703

MYTHS OF THE
NATIVE
AMERICANS

Herald McKinley

Cavendish
Square

New York

Published in 2016 by Cavendish Square Publishing, LLC
243 5th Avenue, Suite 136, New York, NY 10016

First Edition

Website: cavendishsq.com

This publication represents the opinions and views of the author based on his or her personal experience, knowledge, and research. The information in this book serves as a general guide only. The author and publisher have used their best efforts in preparing this book and disclaim liability rising directly or indirectly from the use and application of this book.

CPSIA Compliance Information: Batch #CW16CSQ

All websites were available and accurate when this book was sent to press.

Library of Congress Cataloging-in-Publication Data

McKinley, Herald.
Myths of the Native Americans / Herald McKinley.
pages cm. — (World mythologies)
Includes bibliographical references and index.
ISBN 978-1-5026-0990-8 (hardcover) — ISBN 978-1-5026-0991-5 (ebook)
1. Indian mythology—United States—Juvenile literature. 2. Indian mythology—Canada—Juvenile literature. I. Title.
E98.R3M347 2015
398.2089'97—dc23
015027441

Editorial Director: David McNamara
Editor: Amy Hayes
Copy Editor: Rebecca Rohan
Art Director: Jeffrey Talbot
Designer: Joseph Macri
Senior Production Manager: Jennifer Ryder-Talbot
Production Editor: Renni Johnson
Photo Research: J8 Media

The photographs in this book are used by permission and through the courtesy of: Andrea Izzotti/Shutterstock.com, cover; Brock, Henry Matthew/Private Collection/Bridgeman Images, 4; Catlin, George/Private Collection/Peter Newark Western Americana/Bridgeman Images, 8-9; MyLoupe/UIG Via Getty Images, 10; Nedra Westwater/Age Fotostock, 13; Curtis, Edward Sheriff/Library of Congress,W ashington D.C., USA/The Stapleton Collection/Bridgeman Images, 17; Ann Ronan Pictures/Print Collector/Getty Images, 20; Catlin, George/Bibliotheque Nationale, Paris, France/Bridgeman Images, 23; Bobbi Onia/Underwood Archives/Getty Images, 26; Lewis Spence, Jack, James/Private Collection/The Stapleton Collection/Bridgeman Images, 28; Adam Clark Vroman/Buyenlarge/Getty Images, 37; Marilyn Angel Wynn/Getty Images, 40; Brooklyn Museum, 42; Nancy Carter/North Wind Picture Archives, 44; Joe Mabel/ Burke Museum totem poles 01.jpg/Wikimedia Commons, 46; Werner Forman Archive/Bridgeman Images, 49; Werner Forman Archive/Age Fotostock, 51; MPI/Getty Images, 54; Robert Bird/Alamy, 58; Private Collection/De Agostini Picture Library/Bridgeman Images, 60; Werner Forman/Universal Images Group/Getty Images, 62; NativeStock/North Wind Picture Archives, 66; Nancy G Western Photography, Nancy Greifenhagen/Alamy, 68; Public Domain/Lidded trinket and trade baskets, Hupa Karuk Yurok – Mount Shasta Sisson Museum - DSC02808.JPG/Wikimedia Commons, 71; Mallardg500/Getty Images, 74; Universal Images Group via Getty Images, 79.

Printed in the United States of America

TABLE OF

CONTENTS

The Importance of Mythology

Native Americans passed down myths
and traditions by telling stories.

From folk heroes to gods, campfires to cathedrals, **myths** are stories that are told over and over again. These important stories deepen the identity and customs of a culture. Myths shaped the lives of the people who heard them. These timeless tales of a civilization's gods and heroes were a part of the beliefs, values, and practices of people who lived long ago.

What makes a story a myth? Unlike a narrative written by a particular author, a myth is a traditional story that has been handed down from generation to generation, first orally and later in written form. Nearly all myths tell the deeds of gods, goddesses, and other divine beings. These age-old tales were once widely accepted as true and sacred. Their primary purpose was to explain the mysteries of life and the origins of a society's customs, institutions, and religious rituals.

Mythology (the whole collection of myths belonging to a society) played an important role in ancient cultures. In very early times, people created myths to explain the awe-inspiring, uncontrollable forces of nature, such as thunder, lightning, darkness, drought, and death. Even after philosophers and scientists began to develop more rational explanations for these mysteries, myths continued to provide comforting answers to the many questions that could never be fully solved. People of all cultures have asked the same basic questions about the world around them, such as how did the world begin, what is the purpose of living, and what happens after death?

The myths of the different **tribes** of Native Americans are often funny, strange, and full of adventure. There is trickery, wisdom, and folly. These myths were not just

An Apache man marks the ground as others look on.

created out of people's imaginations. A civilization's geography, government, and culture all influence what stories are told, and which stories eventually become myth. Native Americans had heroes and **tricksters** who participated in origin stories. The origin stories they passed down from generation to generation instilled a strong respect for nature and animals.

Mythology serves as instruction, inspiration, and entertainment. Well-known stories offer people in a society a way to express their fundamental beliefs and values and communicate these beliefs to future generations.

Myths preserve and embellish tales of a civilization's accomplishments and teach important lessons about conduct and priorities. These captivating stories provided enjoyment to countless listeners and readers in ancient times, just as they do today.

"Indian" or "Native American?"

When Christopher Columbus arrived in the Americas in 1492, he thought that he had reached the Southeast Asian islands known to Europeans as the Indies. Because of his mistake, the Native peoples of the New World became known as "Indians." In the 1960s, historians substituted the more accurate term "Native Americans." Today, there is some disagreement among America's Native peoples over which is the more acceptable term. Some people choose "Native American." Others favor the more familiar "Indian" or "American Indian," rejecting "Native American" as a term imposed by white historians without the Native peoples' consent. Most prefer to be referred to by their specific tribe, such as **Blackfoot** or **Cherokee**. This book respectfully uses both "Native American" and "Indian" when speaking of the original peoples of North America in general. Those terms do not include the original inhabitants of Alaska, such as the **Inuit** and Aleuts, who are usually known as Alaskan Natives.

MYTHS OF THE NATIVE AMERICANS

PART 1:
Who Were the Peoples of North America?

The Geography of Native American Cultures

This is a Lenape longhouse. The Lenape and many other tribes made longhouses for homes and gathering places.

According to anthropologists, prehistoric hunters began to migrate from Asia to the North American continent about forty thousand years ago. These hunting parties traveled over an ice mass called the Bering Strait during the last ice age. As the centuries wore on, these early peoples spread throughout the Western Hemisphere, establishing a rich tapestry of civilizations. These people became the Native Americans of North America and were organized into many different tribes.

The Native American tribes were scattered across an immense continent with a remarkable variety of climates and landscapes. In the far north of North America lie the ice and tundra (cold treeless plains) of the Arctic. Parts of the south are hot and tropical. In between these extremes are mountain ranges, plateaus, grassy plains, dense woodlands, dry deserts, and broad river valleys.

North America's Native cultures were as varied as the continent. A tribe's way of life—including its food, clothing, shelter, tools, arts and crafts, and social organization—was shaped by the resources and challenges of the natural environment. In the fertile woodlands of the Northeast, people often lived in large, well-organized farming villages. Their homes included wooden **longhouses** and **wigwams** covered with bark or woven reeds. In the Great Plains, small hunting bands followed the vast wandering herds of buffalo. These **nomadic** hunters lived in tepees made of poles covered with buffalo hides, which were easy to transport from place to place.

Men and women would work side by side to help construct longhouses.

The mythology of different tribes was deeply affected by their natural environments. Native American myths vary widely from culture to culture and tribe to tribe, but all of the traditional tales reflect a deep respect for nature. Hunting tribes have stories about the origins of the buffalo and other game animals. Farming cultures mythologized the gift of corn and other cultivated plants. Stories of the Arctic often centered on the sea and the powerful spirits who controlled the supply of sea animals.

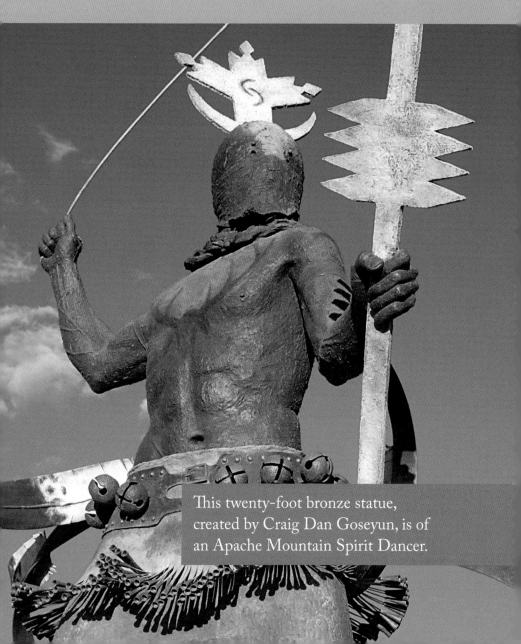

The Regions of the Tribes

This twenty-foot bronze statue, created by Craig Dan Goseyun, is of an Apache Mountain Spirit Dancer.

North America is a huge continent. It had large amounts of land for different cultures to develop. Before Europeans began to colonize, North America was home to hundreds of tribes. These tribes were spread across the land, and in total, Native peoples were speaking three hundred or more separate languages. Unfortunately, there are not many written records about each tribe.

To make it more manageable to study all these different peoples, scholars divided the continent into geographical regions known as culture areas. The different tribes within a particular culture area often developed similar lifestyles as they adapted to the same kind of environment.

One commonly accepted system divides North America into ten culture areas: Arctic, Subarctic, Northeast, Southeast, Great Plains, Northwest Coast, Plateau, California, Great Basin, and Southwest. The map on page 15 shows the approximate borders of these regions. Several of the tribes from each culture area are listed on page 16. This book covers at least one myth from each of the ten regions and includes information about the people who gave these ancient stories life.

NATIVE AMERICAN CULTURE AREAS

BEAUFORT SEA

NORTHWEST COAST

ARCTIC

SUBARCTIC

PACIFIC OCEAN

PLATEAU

GREAT PLAINS

GREAT BASIN

CALIFORNIA

NORTHEAST

ATLANTIC OCEAN

SOUTHEAST

SOUTHWEST

CARIBBEAN SEA

N

KILOMETERS
0   1,000

0   600
MILES

Tribes Organized by Region

Arctic
Aleut, Inuit

Subarctic
Beaver, Chipewyan, Cree, Dogrib, Innu, Northern **Ojibwa**, Slavey

Northeast
Abenaki, Delaware, **Iroquois** (including Cayuga, Mohawk, Oneida, Onondaga, and Seneca), Maliseet, Menominee, Micmac, Mohegan, Ojibwa, Passamaquoddy, Shawnee, Wampanoag

Southeast
Caddo, Cherokee, Chickasaw, Choctaw, Creek, Natchez, Seminole

Great Plains
Apache, Arapaho, Blackfoot, Cheyenne, Comanche, Crow, Kiowa, Mandan, Omaha, Osage, Pawnee, **Sioux** (including Dakota, Lakota, and Nakota), Wichita

Northwest Coast
Chinook, Haida, Kwakiutl, Makah, **Tlingit**, Tsimshian

Plateau
Flathead, Kalispel, **Klamath**, **Nez Perce**, Shuswap, Spokane, Yakima

California
Chumash, Karuk, Maidu, Miwok, Pomo, Wiyot, Yurok

Great Basin
Bannock, **Paiute**, Shoshone, Ute, Washoe

Southwest
Mohave, Navajo, Papago, Pima, **Pueblo** (including Acoma, **Hopi**, Taos, and **Zuni**), Yaqui

A Variety of Cultures

These Atsina are dressed in warriors' clothing, prepared for battle.

E very tribe had its own lifestyle, its own customs, its own traditions. Because of this, it is impossible to describe "Native American culture." Instead of listing an inventory of differences, however, we can point to some features of daily life that were shared by many of North America's Native peoples.

Native American society was generally organized around family. Often the members of a **clan** (extended family) lived together in a village. Villages in areas rich in natural resources might include hundreds or even thousands of people. In less bountiful regions such as the Arctic, settlements might consist of just two or three married couples and their children. Large settlements often broke up into small separate camps during the winter months, reuniting for the summer hunting season. There were also a number of nomadic tribes who roamed the land in small bands, searching for game animals, seeds, nuts, and other food.

Neighboring villages sometimes formed loose alliances for hunting, trading, religious ceremonies, and warfare. Alliances were governed by councils made up of representatives from each village. The villages in an alliance retained their own independent governments, usually ruled by an elected chief and council.

The lives of most American Indians revolved around seasonal farming and hunting activities. Important crops included maize (corn), beans, and squash. The Indians developed sophisticated methods for hunting and trapping game animals such as buffalo, caribou, and deer. In northern coastal regions, hunters used spears and harpoons to capture seals, walruses, whales, and other sea animals.

Tribes in many regions also used nets, traps, hooks, and spears to gather fish from lakes, rivers, and the sea.

In terms of gender roles, Native Americans traditionally separated men's and women's work. Men took care of the hunting, fishing, trading, and warfare. Women tended to the crops, gathered wild plants, cooked, made clothing and other household items, and cared for the children.

In tribes in North America, women enjoyed considerable respect and authority. Many Native tribes were matrilineal, meaning that possessions and titles were inherited through the mother's side of the family. Some tribes were matriarchies, meaning that women held all the traditional roles of power. However, many cultures viewed both sexes as equal. Among the Iroquois, for example, women had the power to elect government leaders and veto council decisions. In mythology, women were often honored as the life-giving force to future generations.

A Strong Connection to Nature

This is a Sioux war dance. Many tribes held religious ceremonies lasting several days before they would go off to war.

The religions of the Native American peoples were as complex and varied as the peoples themselves. Each had their own gods, their own ceremonies, and their own ways of worship. However, most Indians shared some basic beliefs about the importance of the mysterious forces of the world around them. In this brief look at those age-old religions, we have used the past tense. Keep in mind, though, that many American Indians today still follow the spiritual beliefs and practices of their ancestors, and that many of these religions are very much alive.

Most Native cultures honored a Great Spirit, known by a host of different names, including Wakan Tanka (to the Lakota Sioux), Tirawahat (to the Pawnee), and Gitche Manitou (to the Micmac, Ojibwa, and others). The Great Spirit was loving and merciful, all-knowing and all-powerful. He created the world, and he was present in all people, places, and things. In addition, Native Americans honored the Earth as the source of all life. In the words of one nineteenth-century chief, "The Great Spirit is our Father, but the Earth is our Mother."

Each Native community also recognized a multitude of lesser spirits. Every natural thing—from plants, animals, and people to water, stones, the air, and the stars—had its own spirit. Along with all the nature spirits, there might be ghosts dwelling near the village graveyard and sprites inhabiting local lakes or rocks. Humans were just one part of the enormous sacred circle of life. They were not meant to rule over the rest of creation. Instead, they were responsible for honoring the Earth and caring for all its creatures.

In this drawing, explorers from the West watch a Native American stag sacrifice.

The Indians' attitude towards animals reflected the sense of kinship they felt with all creation. According to Native American myths, people and animals once spoke together, sharing their thoughts and ideas. Although animals had lost their ability to talk, they still cared about their human brothers and sisters. That was why the buffalo, the deer, and other animals allowed themselves to be hunted. Ancient stories such as "The Zuni Tale of the Corn Maidens" (page 37) and "Disease and Medicine of the Cherokee" (page 77) served as reminders to be thankful for all of the gifts of nature.

Spirituality in Everything

A group of Native Americas perform a buffalo dance.

The religious beliefs of Native Americans impacted every area of people's lives. Indians were aware of them while hunting, gathering, working, and playing. Through their customs, rituals, and stories, they honored the spirits and asked for their blessings and protection.

Indian hunters performed rituals to thank the animals for their sacrifice and honor their spirits. Farmers gave prayers of thanksgiving for the gifts shared by the sacred Earth. Prayers might include words, songs, gestures, dancing, and offerings of tobacco, considered one of the most sacred plants.

Special prayers and rituals were performed at certain times during the farming and hunting seasons. The entire community joined together to celebrate occasions such as the planting and the harvest, the seasonal whale or buffalo hunt, and the annual return of the salmon. These grand ceremonies could last days or even weeks. For example, the annual Corn Dance of the Pueblo peoples included several days of fasting, feasting, dancing, prayers, and other observances.

In many tribes an honored man or woman known as a shaman acted as a link between the community and the spirit world. Shamans were believed to have special powers that made it possible for them to communicate directly with the spirits of animals, plants, or the dead. Through prayers, songs, and rituals, they asked the spirits to help the community in times of need. Shamans also used plants, herbs, and ritual objects such as sacred pipes and rattles to treat the sick and injured.

Religious rituals and mythology were closely intertwined. Shamans recited or acted out myths as they performed their magic. Elders and other respected members of the community passed down sacred knowledge through the ancient stories of their people. Many Native American myths took five or six hours to tell. The storyteller paused frequently to gesture, sing, beat a drum, or allow listeners to respond with a "yes" or a laugh. Important words and phrases were repeated over and over to highlight their meaning.

These long spoken narratives, intended to be told around a group of listeners, lose much of their power when they are translated from the original language, shortened, and put down in writing. Many tribes are trying to keep their stories alive in their original form, teaching their language so that their children can hear the words as they were meant to be heard for generations to come. Other languages have been lost to time. Yet recording the age-old tales also helps preserve them for future generations and makes them available to all.

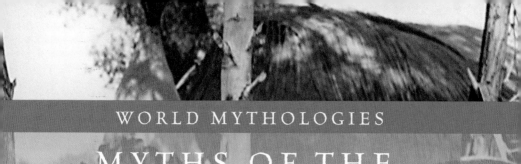

WORLD MYTHOLOGIES

MYTHS OF THE
NATIVE
AMERICANS

PART 2:
Stories and Myths

From Sky to Earth, the Iroquois Creation Story

An illustration shows two earth divers as they reach the bottom of the sea.

Each Native American culture has its own creation story, its own tales of the first humans to walk the Earth. These tales vary significantly from culture to culture and are often influenced by a tribe's way of life and natural environment. Even within a tribe, there are often many different versions of the same myth. This is because over time, storytellers added their own interpretations and details to old tales, creating a rich variety of creation tales.

Some Native American creation stories feature a powerful god or goddess who shapes the world and everything in it. Other accounts give credit to two creators. These might be twin brothers, sisters, a man and woman, a father and son, or a pair of animals. Ancient tales from the Southwest say that the first people climbed through a series of dying underworlds to reach the present Earth. In accounts from the Northwest, people descend to the world through a hole in the sky. One of the most common creation stories, found all over North America, tells of a time when the world was covered by an endless black sea. An animal known as the **earth diver** goes to the bottom of the sea to scoop up mud, which becomes the Earth.

This version of the earth diver story is a blending of traditional creation tales told by the Iroquois. The Iroquois were the most powerful group of Indians in the Northeast culture area. The group originally included five **nations** that joined together to form a confederacy, or political union: the Cayuga, Mohawk, Oneida, Onondaga, and Seneca. (A sixth nation, the Tuscarora, joined the confederacy in 1714.) The people of the Iroquois nations were skilled farmers who grew corn, beans, and squash. They also hunted deer, moose, bear, and other game animals and fished in the region's many lakes and rivers.

The Iroquois called themselves the **Haudenosaunee**, which means "people building a longhouse." The name came from their longhouses, large wood-and-bark buildings that each lodged twenty or more related families. On long winter nights, the families would gather around the longhouse fire to hear an elder tell the ancient tales of their people. Some stories spoke of gods, heroes, revered animals, and the powerful spirits who dwelt in the fields, forests, lakes, and rivers. Some explained the origins of special customs and ceremonies. Others related the very beginnings of our world, which the Haudenosaunee call Turtle Island.

Dramatis Personae

Dramatis Personae is a Latin phrase meaning "persons of the drama," or cast of characters. Here are the characters who play a role in this creation story:

Muskrat Powerful swimmer who brings up mud used to create the world

Turtle Revered animal who supports the world on his back

Aataentsic (at-uh-EN-sik) Sky goddess and mother of humanity, also known as Sky Woman

On a Turtle's Back

They say that once, a long time ago, the Earth was covered by a great black sea. There was no land, only muddy water. There was no sun or moon or stars, only darkness. The only creatures in this gloomy world were the animals who live in the water, such as the Loon, Muskrat, Beaver, Mink, and Turtle.

Far above the Earth was a land in the sky. The beings who dwelt in the Sky World had everything they needed. Their forests were full of game, and their lakes and streams teemed with fish. Their fields produced an endless harvest of vegetables. The people were so happy that there was never any sickness, and no one ever died.

A sacred tree stood in the center of a village in the Sky World. Near the tree was a great lodge. In the lodge dwelt a chief and his wife, Aataentsic, or Sky Woman, who was expecting a child. One night Sky Woman had a dream. She dreamed that the great tree was uprooted. When she told her dream to her husband, he was deeply saddened. The branches of the tree gave fruit to the people. Its blossoms popped open each morning, bringing them daylight. But the chief knew that dreams are a window into the spirit world. His wife had clearly had a dream of great power, and it would be dangerous to ignore such an omen.

So the chief ordered the people to dig up the great tree. That left a gaping hole where the roots had gone into the floor of the Sky World. Sky Woman stood on the edge of the hole. She leaned over to peer down at the lower world. All of a sudden she lost her balance. She reached out and desperately clutched at the tree branches. The seeds came away in her hands. Then she fell through the hole in the sky, into darkness.

Down and down she drifted, twisting and turning like a leaf in the breeze. Far below Muskrat raised his head above the muddy waters. "What is that way up there, flying down to us?" he cried.

The other animals looked up in amazement. "It is a human falling from above," called Loon. "We must help her."

Swiftly a pair of swans flew into the air. They joined their wings together, and Sky Woman came to rest on their soft white backs. Then Turtle called a council. "The swans cannot carry their burden forever," he said. "We must make a dry place for the woman to live. I can support her on my back. Who will fetch soil from the bottom of the sea to make a platform?"

Otter was the first to speak. "I am a strong swimmer. I will find some soil beneath the water." So Otter dived down into the sea. He swam and swam, but he could not reach the bottom.

Then it was Loon's turn. "I dive a long way to catch my food," he said. "I will try to bring up soil for the woman." So Loon plunged into the water. He swam down and down, even farther than Otter. He dived so deep that he nearly drowned, but he could not reach the bottom.

Next, Beaver took a turn. Then Mink and Duck and Toad and many other animals dived beneath the sea.

One by one, the animals swam down far beneath the surface. One by one, they came back exhausted and empty-handed. It seemed that there was no way to fetch soil from the bottom of the water.

At last Muskrat stood before the company. "I will bring back soil or die trying," he vowed. He plunged beneath the water. Down, down, down he swam. He was gone for so long that the others were afraid he would never return. Finally his body floated to the surface. The brave little animal's breath had failed him.

But what was that? Muskrat's small paws were clenched around something. The animals pried open his right paw. There they found a bit of mud, scratched from the bottom of the water.

Quickly, they placed the mud on Turtle's back. Gently, the swans lowered Sky Woman to the new foundation. There was just enough room for her to stand with one foot on top of the other. Then a strange thing happened. The soil began to grow. Little by little, it grew until there was room for the woman to lie down on it. Little by little, it stretched out until she could walk around on it. Before long, the soil had grown into a great island in the middle of the water.

Sky Woman opened her hands. She scattered the seeds that she had brought from the Sky World. Grasses and bushes and trees sprang up on the newly formed Earth. The woman took some bark from the trees and built herself a shelter. And there she lived contentedly.

In time, Sky Woman gave birth to a baby girl. Her daughter grew up to become the mother of twin boys.

The Orphan of the Sea

The Inuit live along the Arctic coast, from northern Alaska to Greenland. Their homeland is beautiful but forbidding, with long, bitter-cold winters and scarce resources. The myths of the Inuit reflect their harsh environment and their dependence on the sea. According to one traditional tale, an orphan girl named Sedna was left behind when the people of her village moved to new hunting grounds during a famine. As the villagers left the shore, the friendless child jumped into the water and clung to the edges of their boats. The people chopped off her fingers, one by one. The fingers fell into the sea, where they were transformed into the seals, whales, and other sea animals. Sedna lived on beneath the sea as the animals' keeper.

In the early 1920s, Danish explorer Knud Rasmussen collected Inuit stories and songs during an Arctic expedition. This hunting song came from the Netsilik, a group of Inuit living in one of the bleakest and most remote parts of the Arctic. The Netsilik name for Sedna is Nuliajuk.

O sea goddess Nuliajuk,
when you were a little unwanted orphan girl
we let you drown.
You fell in the water
and when you hung onto the kayaks crying
we cut off your fingers.
So you sank into the sea
and your fingers turned into
the innumerable seals.

You sweet orphan Nuliajuk,
I beg you now
bring me a gift,
not anything from the land
but a gift from the sea,
something that will make a nice soup.
Dare I say it right out?
I want a seal!

You dear little orphan,
creep out of the water
panting on this beautiful shore,
puh, puh, like this, puh, puh,
O welcome gift
in the shape of a seal!

These two magical brothers would complete the work of creation. They would make the rivers and rapids, the flowers and thorns, the helpful game animals and the fierce, dangerous beasts. They would fashion the first man and woman from clay and bring them to life.

> They placed the earth on the back of the Turtle.
>
> ~ John Buck, Onondaga

The Turtle still carries the world on his back, and the descendants of the Sky Woman still walk upon it. When Turtle is restless, he moves his feet and stretches his limbs. His movements cause the seas to swell and earthquakes to rumble.

The Zuni Tale of the Corn Maidens

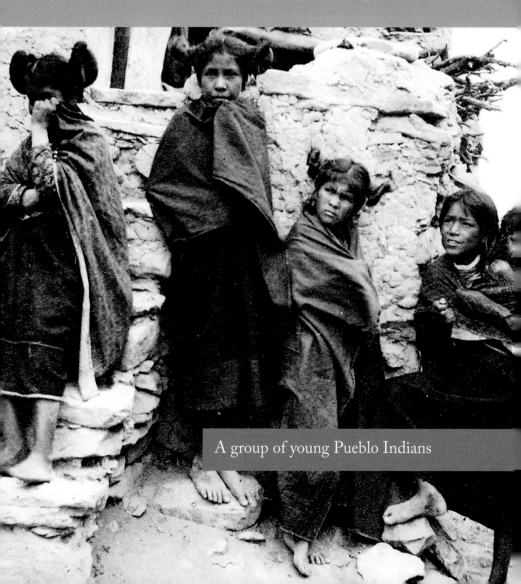

A group of young Pueblo Indians

Native Americans have a wide variety of origin stories. Similar to creation myths, origin stories are tales about the beginnings of animals, plants, the seasons, day and night, good and evil, and tribal customs and ceremonies. However, it is important to remember that origin stories are more than simply accounts of how things came into existence. Like all myths, they are stories that inspire listeners to reflect on the mysteries of nature and the world around them.

Origin stories and other myths have always been especially important in the lives of the Pueblo peoples. The Pueblos were the first inhabitants of the deserts and plateaus of the American Southwest. They lived in large villages made up of stone and adobe (mud-brick) homes that looked a lot like modern-day apartment buildings. They were skilled farmers who coaxed the dry sandy soil into producing many different kinds of corn, in various sizes, textures, and colors. Many of their sacred stories honored the powerful spirits who controlled the rain and the growth of crops. Today the descendants of the ancient Pueblos, including the Hopi, Taos, and Zuni, still perform traditional ceremonies designed to ensure rainfall, abundant harvests, and good fortune. At the heart of their ceremonies are stories reaching back hundreds of years. Narrated by tribal elders and acted out by tribal dancers, these ancient tales help preserve the peoples' history, values, and spiritual beliefs.

> Before corn was created, all the people lived on the seeds that were gathered.
>
> ~ Frank Goldtooth, Navajo

One of the most important Zuni ceremonies is Molawai, a dramatic retelling of the myth of the Corn Maidens. To the people of Pueblo cultures, corn is not only an important food crop but also a sacred symbol of life and fertility. The Corn Maidens were the source of corn. The story of their loss and recovery teaches the importance of honoring the spirits for their great gifts.

Dramatis Personae

Corn Maidens Six immortal sisters who were the source of corn

Payatamu Pueblo spirit of the dawn, dew, and music

The Ungrateful Scree and the Corn Maidens

When the world was new, only grasses grew on our mother, the Earth. The children of Earth had nothing to eat but the seeds that they gathered from the grasses. Those were hungry times!

Then the Great Father took pity on the people. He sent the Corn Maidens to help them. The six beautiful sisters danced in the grassy fields. Wherever they danced, plants sprouted and grew tall. The silken tassels waved in the summer winds, and when the people peeled back the leaves, they found big, golden, delicious ears of corn.

Now there was plenty to eat. The Corn Maidens dwelt among the children of Earth, and all was peace and happiness. But as time went by, the people began to forget how much they owed the immortal sisters. They became wasteful, growing more corn than they needed.

A Zuni kachina doll representing a corn maiden

They tore the ripe ears roughly from the plants and tossed them into dirty storerooms. They let the extra corn rot in the fields or piled it up like garbage. When the time for the yearly dance of the Corn Maidens drew near, some people even complained that they were getting sick and tired of the same old celebrations.

Finally, it was the night of the Corn Dance. The people had built a great shelter of branches in the center of the village. As darkness gathered, the drums sounded. The Corn Maidens wound their way along the path from the river toward the village. How graceful were the movements of these blessed spirits! How the firelight sparkled on their white garments as they danced beneath the leafy shelter! Everyone who saw them sighed at their loveliness. But as the night wore on, some of the young warriors grew bold. They stared so intently that the maidens blushed and lowered their eyes. The men left the circle of watchers to join the spirits. Closer and closer they danced. One young warrior even reached out and tried to touch the hand of the eldest sister.

The Corn Maidens were saddened to see that the people no longer held them precious. They wept as they danced, and their tears became a thick white mist, hiding them from view. At last, the beautiful maidens wrapped their long white cloaks around them and vanished.

In the morning, when the people of the village saw that the Corn Maidens had left, they just shrugged. No matter! There was plenty of corn. They kept up their wasteful ways, and by spring, there was very little seed corn left in the storehouse. The people planted what they had, but the harvest was slim. The next year was even harder. The year after that, the pale plants withered and died in the fields. The people had to go back to gathering seeds from the wild grasses. Soon, even those grew scarce.

Finally, the village elders called a council. "Our foolishness has driven away the Corn Maidens," they said. "We must find them and beg for their forgiveness."

Two young warriors were chosen for the difficult task. They searched and searched, until they came to a mountain. Up they climbed, and there at the top was the nest of the sacred Eagle.

"Scree! What is it?" asked the Eagle, snapping his beak.

"Our beautiful Corn Maidens have vanished, and we are starving," said the warriors.

"Nothing escapes my keen eye," said the Eagle. "I will find them before the day is over." Then he launched himself into the sky. He circled higher and higher, until he appeared smaller than a drop of rain in a whirlwind. North and east and west the Eagle scanned the Earth, but he could find no trace of the Corn Maidens.

So the warriors went to seek the Hawk. They searched and searched, until they found him perched on an anthill.

"Chi-chi-chi! What is it?" asked the Hawk, ruffling his feathers.

"We are searching for our Corn Maidens," said the warriors. "Your brother the Eagle cannot find them."

"Of course he can't!" laughed the bird. "He soars too high above the clouds." Then the Hawk rose into the air. North and east and west he darted. He skimmed over the tops of the forests and hedgerows, but he could find no trace of the Corn Maidens.

So the warriors went to seek the Crow. They searched and searched, until they found him pecking at a heap of garbage.

"Caw caw! What is it?" asked the Crow, ruffling up his black collar.

A statue of Payatamu

"We are seeking our Corn Maidens," said the warriors. "Your brothers the Eagle and the Hawk cannot find them."

"Of course they can't!" said the Crow. "Everyone knows that only I can hunt out even the tiniest grub or beetle! I will help you, but first you must take me to your village."

So the two warriors led the Crow to the village. But when the sly bird spied the last ear of corn in the storehouse, he swooped down and snatched it up in his claws. "I guess this is the last you'll ever see of your maidens," he called mockingly as he flew off with it.

All the men of the village shouted. All the women wailed. Then, suddenly, they heard the sound of a flute. A masked figure came strolling up the path from the river. It was Payatamu, god of the dawn, who sprinkles the dew to freshen the earth each morning. The merry god had heard the people weeping. He saw that they were truly sorry for having offended the Corn Maidens. With a smile, he told the elders to prepare four **prayer sticks** decorated with soft white down from the Eagle. He planted the sticks in the ground. He knelt and watched. The feathers fluttered gently from the south toward the north, just as though someone were breathing on them.

"Aha!" cried Payatamu. "The breath of the Corn Maidens!" Swift as the wind, the god flew south to the Land of Everlasting Summer. There, he found the six sisters sleeping at the bottom of a deep blue lake.

Payatamu pulled out his magic flute. He played a merry tune. His music snaked through the air and wiggled its way to the bottom of the water. The Corn Maidens stirred and awoke. They rose from the water to the dry land. They picked up their empty baskets. Then they followed the god to the village, where the people greeted them joyfully.

As the villagers watched, Payatamu turned to the eldest Corn Maiden. He lifted the basket from her head. She smiled and faded from view. The people opened her basket and saw that it was overflowing with yellow seed corn. Then the god lifted each basket in turn from the heads of the other maidens. Each sister smiled and vanished. Their baskets, too, were filled with seed corn, one of each color: blue, red, white, speckled, and black.

Hopi corn dancers

"The Corn Maidens have brought you their gifts once more," Payatamu told the villagers. "Treasure them, and you will never know hunger." Then he vanished like the morning dew and was never seen again. But he left behind his magic flute, so the people could always make music for the Corn Dance.

To this day, the sisters have lived in the Land of Everlasting Summer. Their sweet breath warms the earth and brings rain clouds to the sky every spring. The stalks grow tall, and the corn ripens. Every year, the children of Earth have honored the Corn Maidens with songs and dances. They thank the Corn Maidens for their bounty and treasure their gifts.

The Nez Perce and the Beaver

The Nez Perce traveled across the forests and canyons of the Plateau region. Their diet included wild roots and berries; elk, deer, and other game animals; and fish from the rivers and streams. Nez Perce tribal elders told many tales about the beginnings of day and night, the stars, and the animals. One of their origin stories gives Beaver credit for the valuable gift of fire.

The pine trees had the secret of fire and guarded it jealously, so that no matter how cold it was, they alone could warm themselves. At length an unusually cold winter came, and all the animals were in danger of freezing to death. But all their attempts to discover the pines' secret were in vain, until Beaver at last hit upon a plan. ...

The pines were about to hold a great council. They had built a large fire to warm themselves after bathing in the icy water, and sentinels were posted to prevent intruders from stealing their fire secret. But Beaver had hidden under the bank near the fire before the sentries had taken their places, and when a live coal rolled down the bank, he seized it, hid it in his breast, and ran away as fast as he could.

The pines immediately raised a hue and cry and started after him. ... There was one cedar running in the forefront of the pines. ... He ran to the top of the hill and saw Beaver just diving into [a river]. Further pursuit was out of the question. The cedar stood and watched Beaver dart across [the river] and give fire to some willows on the opposite bank, and recross farther on and give fire to the birches, and so on to several other kinds of trees. Since then, all who have wanted fire have got it from these particular trees, because they have fire in them and give it up readily when their wood is rubbed together in the ancient way.

Tlingit and Tismishian Raven Tales

Twentieth-century
reproductions of
nineteenth-century
Tsimshian and Haida
totem poles

L ike many cultures around the world, Native Americans were fascinated by the sky. The sun, moon, and stars were very important. The sun marked the hours of the day. The phases of the moon and the movement of the constellations set the time for planting, harvesting, hunting, and special ceremonies. As well as being useful guides for telling time and marking the seasons, the sun, moon, and stars were an important part of Native American myth.

Many Indian myths accounted for the origins of the heavenly bodies. Some tales said that the sun, moon, and stars were made by a powerful creator god or goddess. In other stories, a remarkable animal was responsible for bringing light to the dark world. According to several Northwest Coast tribes, that heroic figure was Raven.

The Northwest Coast stretches along the Pacific Ocean from northern California to Alaska. Native tribes of this region include the Haida, Tsimshian, and Tlingit. These early peoples enjoyed an abundance of food from the sea, including salmon, seals, and other fish and sea mammals. The pine and cedar forests abounded with deer, elk, black bears, and other game animals. Wood from the forests went into the Indians' large plank houses, dugout canoes, and beautifully carved totem poles.

In the summertime, life on the Northwest Coast revolved around hunting, fishing, and gathering roots and berries. The long winter months were a time for woodworking, basket weaving, and other crafts. Special occasions such as a child's naming day or the inheritance of a chief's title and territories were celebrated with elaborate ceremonies called potlatches. During a potlatch, the host showered his guests with gifts to demonstrate his wealth and importance. The festivities included a huge feast, dramatic masked dancing, and storytelling. Some of the most popular stories told the adventures of Raven. In this tale from the Tlingit and Tsimshian peoples, we learn how Raven captured the light of the sun, moon, and stars.

Dramatis Personae

Raven Part-human, part-bird hero who brings light to the world

Raven Steals the Light

A long time ago, the world lay in blackness. A rich chief in a village by a stream kept all the light for himself, while the people of other villages stumbled around in the dark. The men could not see to hunt or fish. The women could not see to gather the wild roots and berries. Mothers even had a hard time feeding their children. Everyone was sad and hungry.

The chief of one of the dark villages was determined to get light for his people. This chief happened to have a very beautiful daughter. One day he called a meeting. He pledged to give his daughter in marriage to any warrior who could bring light to the world. There were many volunteers. The villagers sang the praises of the warriors as they set out from the village. But not one of the young men returned. Some people said that they had found the road too hard. Others believed that the seekers had reached the land of light and decided to stay there.

The chief was discouraged, but he did not give up. He kept holding his meetings and calling for volunteers. Finally, at one meeting, his call was answered with silence. Not one young man stepped forward. Then Raven stood and addressed the company. He gave a long speech, in which he bragged about his courage and cleverness. He ended his speech with these words: "I will bring you light."

This ceremonial headdress depicts a raven.

All the people laughed at the boastful bird. They whooped and hooted so loudly that the building shook. But the chief called for silence. He had no more faith in Raven's promise than anyone else, but he was not about to let any chance of finding light pass by, no matter how slim. So the wise leader praised Raven for his noble resolve. He encouraged the bird to be steadfast and strong. And he reminded Raven of the great prize that awaited him if he succeeded.

Early the next morning, Raven flew away from the village. He flew for days and days in the pitch darkness. At last he saw a glimmer of light on the horizon. Following the light, he came to a large and prosperous village. The light in this village was so bright that it was almost blinding.

Raven saw that the light came from the largest house in the village. He flew to a high branch in a tree overlooking the shining house. He waited and waited.

At last the rich chief's daughter emerged, carrying a wooden bowl. The maiden walked toward the stream. Raven flew ahead quickly. Using his magic powers, he changed himself into a little green leaf and fluttered down into the stream. When the girl knelt by the water, the leaf floated into her bowl. When she tilted her head to drink, she swallowed the tiny leaf along with the water.

Nine months later, the chief's daughter gave birth to a son. The child had hair like shiny feathers. He had small black eyes and a long hooked nose like a bird's beak. It was Raven, born as a baby boy!

The Raven-baby was the firstborn son of the chief's daughter, and so he was pampered and spoiled. Everyone wanted to wash him and feed him and cuddle him. When he cried, everyone rushed to give him whatever he wanted. As soon as he could crawl, the baby began to creep around the house, pointing and crying. He pointed at a pipe. His mother gave him the pipe. He pointed at a basket. His grandmother gave him the basket. Within a few days, he had handled everything in the house. Everything except three carved wooden boxes belonging to his grandfather.

"Ga! Ga!" wailed the baby, pointing at the smallest box.

"What does my precious little grandson want?" asked the chief. "Look, he's pointing at the box of stars. Quick, give it to him so he'll stop crying."

So the mother gave the Raven-baby the smallest box. He turned it over and over in his little hands. He knocked on the lid and pushed it around on the floor. Then, when no one was looking, he threw it against the wall. Smash! The box cracked open, and all the stars flew up through the smoke hole in the roof, arranging themselves in the sky.

"Ga! Ga! Gaaa!" howled the baby.

"What does my grandson want now?" asked the chief. "He's pointing at the box of the moon. Quick, give it to him before he makes himself sick with crying."

So the mother gave the Raven-baby the middle box. He pretended to play with it happily. But as soon as no one was looking, he threw it against the wall. Smash! The box shattered, and the moon escaped through the smoke hole, taking its place in the sky.

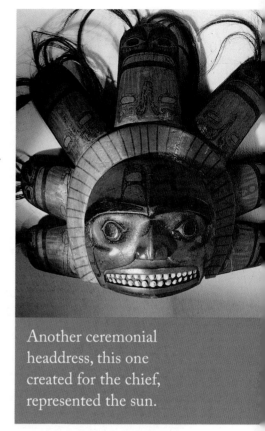

Another ceremonial headdress, this one created for the chief, represented the sun.

"Ga! Gaaa! GAAAAAA!" shrieked the baby.

"What on earth does the child want now?" asked the chief, sticking his fingers in his ears. "Quick, give him the last box. Give him anything to stop that howling!"

So the mother gave the baby the biggest and most beautiful box. He seized the prize with a raucous cry and turned himself back into Raven. The chief shouted, but it was too late. The tricky bird flew up through the smoke hole and escaped from the village.

Raven flew for days and days. Each day it grew darker, until he could hardly see at all. At last he reached his own village. "I have brought you light," said Raven. Then he opened the box. There was a blinding flash, and out burst the sun. All the people went wild with joy and amazement, and the chief kept his promise, giving Raven his daughter in marriage.

> Raven brought order [by] stealing the sun so that humans could see.
>
> ~ Shannon Thunderbird, Tsimshian

It is said that this is how the stars, the moon, and the sun came into the world. How do we know the boastful Raven is telling the truth about the Sun? We need only look at his feathers. Before his adventures the tricky bird was as white as a swan, but when he flew through the smoke hole of the rich chief's house, the soot blackened his feathers. Raven is now as black as the night sky, forever covered in soot.

The Paiute and the North Star

The Paiute lived in the vast dry desert of the Great Basin region. Native peoples traditionally roamed the desert in small family groups. The women gathered pine nuts, seeds, and berries, while the men hunted rabbits, birds, and other small animals. In the plateaus of modern-day Utah, Southern Paiute bands hunted mountain sheep, too. This Southern Paiute tale explains how a mountain sheep named Na-gah became the North Star.

The Paiute and the North Star

Once in the very long ago Na-gah found a very high mountain. Its sides were steep and smooth and its top was a high sharp peak reaching up into the clouds. Na-gah looked up and said, "I wonder what is up there. I will climb to the very highest point."

He set out to find a way up. Around the mountain and around the mountain he went, seeking for a trail, but there was no trail. ...

At last, he found a big crack in the rock that went down and not up. Down into it he went. Soon he found a hole that turned up, and his heart was glad. Up and up he climbed. Soon it grew so dark he could not see, and the cave was full of loose rocks that slipped under his feet and rolled down. ...

When at last Na-gah came out into the open it almost took his breath away. He was on the very top of a very high peak. ... Nowhere could he get down on the outside, and the cave was closed on the inside. "Here," he said, "I must die, but I have climbed my mountain." ...

When [Na-gah's father] Shinob saw him there, he felt sorrowful, for he knew Na-gah could never come down. Shinob said to himself, "... I will not let my brave son die. I will turn him into poot-see, a star, and he can stand there and shine where everyone can see him. ...

It was even so. Na-gah became a star that every living thing can see, and the only star that will always be found in the same place. Directions are set by him and the traveler, looking at him, can always find his way. Always he stands still ... and because he is in the true north, the Indians call him "Qui-am-i Wintook Poot-see," the North Star.

Algonquian Hero Glooscap and the Water Monster

Male members of the Sauk and Fox tribe, which was part of the Algonquian language family

There are many Native American stories that are more like adventure tales than origin myths. They follow main characters referred to as **culture heroes**. Culture heroes can be human beings or animals. They have amazing abilities that allow them to transform other living things, remake the landscape, change shape, and defeat dangerous foes. Culture heroes are often related to origin stories and may be responsible for bringing fire, corn, the buffalo, and other features to the natural world. They also serve as teachers and protectors of the world's first people.

The hero of "Glooscap Slays the Water Monster" comes to us from the **Algonquian** peoples of the Northeast. The Algonquians are a group of independent tribes from several different regions, who speak related languages that all belong to the same "family" of languages (also known as Algonquian). In the Northeast, the Algonquian-speaking tribes include the Abenaki, Maliseet, Micmac, Mohegan, Passamaquoddy, and others. Each of these tribes has its own culture and traditions. In general, the Algonquian way of life was similar in many ways to that of their neighbors, the Iroquois. Most Algonquians were farmers, hunters, and fishermen. They lived in villages governed by tribal councils made up of clan heads, distinguished warriors, or other respected leaders. The traditional dwellings of the northeastern Algonquians were small dome-shaped homes called wigwams.

Glooscap is credited with teaching the Algonquian peoples a variety of skills, including how to fish, hunt, weave, and tan hides. Some stories say that he created the sun and moon, the first people, game animals, and fish.

He also used his great powers to slay giants, monsters, and evil magicians. In this story told by the Micmac, Maliseet, and other Algonquian-speaking tribes of the Northeast, Glooscap matches his powers against a monster who has stolen all the water in the world.

Dramatis Personae

Aglabem Monstrous Bullfrog who steals the world's water

Gitche Manitou Great Spirit who created the world

Glooscap Algonquian culture hero

Glooscap Returns the Water

In olden times, there was a village beside a rushing stream. The people there were very happy. The deer, moose, and caribou gave themselves willingly to the hunters. The forests offered wild plants, berries, and tree sap to make delicious maple syrup. The stream was the only source of water in the land, but it provided the people with all the cool, clear water they needed.

Then came a time when the stream began to fail. It ran low in the summer. In the autumn it was just a trickle, more mud than water. By the spring, the bed of the stream was as dry as the ashes in a cold wigwam fire.

The elders held a council. "We cannot live without water," they said. "We must seek the source of the stream, to find out why it has gone dry."

So a messenger was chosen to travel north to the place where the waters began. The man walked for three days. At last he came to another village, where he saw that a dam had been raised across the stream. The messenger asked the people of the village why they had built the dam. "Our great chief Aglabem wants all the water for himself," they answered.

The man walked to the lake that had been formed by the damming of the stream. There he saw the chief wallowing in the deep water. Aglabem's huge body was bloated and covered with warts. His yellow eyes were like giant pine knots. His mouth was open in a nasty grin that stretched a mile from ear to ear.

"What do you want? What do you want?" croaked the monster.

"My people are thirsty," said the messenger.

"What do I care? What do I care?" croaked Aglabem. Then the monster gave the man a single cup of muddy water to take home to his people.

When the messenger returned with the cup of mud, the people got angry. They decided to send a party of warriors to destroy the dam. The men left the village, bravely singing their death songs. When they reached the dam, Aglabem rose up out of the water. He grabbed the warriors and crushed them with his long, strong fingers. Only one man escaped to return to the village and tell what had happened.

Now the people were in despair. "We cannot defeat a monster!" they cried.

One wise chief spoke up. "We must pray to Gitche Manitou, the Great Spirit," he said. "He will hear our prayers and send us help."

This forty-foot bronze statue of Glooscap stands in front of the Glooscap Heritage Centre in Millbrook, Nova Scotia.

So the people burned their sacred tobacco, and the smoke carried their prayers up to Gitche Manitou. When the Creator heard their pleas, he took pity. He called for his helper Glooscap. He sent the hero down to Earth to help the people.

As soon as Glooscap reached the village, he prepared himself for war. First he made himself twelve feet tall. Then he painted his body as red as blood and drew yellow rings around his eyes. He put one hundred black eagle feathers and one hundred white eagle feathers in his hair. Grabbing a birch tree with one hand, he twisted off a giant war club. Uttering his fearful war cry, he made the mountains tremble. Then Glooscap strode forth from the village, with lightning flashing, thunder booming, and great eagles circling above him.

Just a few giant strides brought Glooscap to the village near the dam. There he saw a young boy. "Bring me water to drink," he commanded.

> [Glooscap] took the shape of a tall warrior, head and shoulders taller than any of the people.
>
> ~ Joseph Bruchac, Abenaki

The boy was frightened of the tall warrior, but he was even more terrified of Aglabem. "I cannot give you water unless the chief commands it," he answered.

"Then go ask your chief," said Glooscap. And he sat down on a log to smoke his pipe. He sat for a long time, until at last the boy returned with a small cup of dirty water.

"I think I will go see your chief myself," said Glooscap. "He will soon give me better water."

So Glooscap continued up the dry streambed until he came to the dam. There he saw the monster lying lazily in the water.

"Give me clean water to drink, you slimy lump of mud!" the hero commanded.

The monster smacked his lips with a noise like thunder. "The waters are mine," he croaked. "Go away, before I swallow you whole!"

"The waters are meant to be shared!" bellowed Glooscap. In his anger he made himself taller than the tallest pine tree. He made himself so wide that even the monster's mile-wide mouth couldn't swallow him. He stamped his foot, and the dam cracked. He struck the dam with his tree club, and it burst open. The waters rushed out in a mighty river, roaring and rolling all the way to the great sea.

Then Glooscap reached down and grabbed the water monster. He squeezed Aglabem with his giant hand. The monster's back bent. His eyes bulged out. He shrank and shrank, until he was nothing but a little bullfrog. "Now you can share the waters with everyone," said Glooscap, and he threw the creature into the river.

Aglabem probably looked much like this American bullfrog when Glooscap was done with him.

Water rushed down the river and filled the dry beds. The thirsty people danced with joy at the sight of all the cold, fresh water. Some jumped into the rushing river. They were so happy to be in the water that they stayed there and turned into fish, crabs, beavers, turtles, and other water-dwelling creatures. The people from that village still live in that river. And so does the bullfrog. If you capture a bullfrog, you can see the wrinkles that were left on his back by Glooscap's fingers.

Nanabush, The Ojibwa Hero

The Ojibwa (also called the Anishinabe or Chippewa) are an Algonquian-speaking people of the Northeast, Great Plains, and Subarctic regions. Like other Subarctic peoples, the Northern Ojibwa lived in small, close-knit family groups. During the long frozen winters, they hunted caribou, moose, bear, and beaver. In the brief warm season, they fished in the lakes and rivers and gathered berries in the forests. They wore sturdy clothing made from moose or caribou hides, decorated with porcupine quills.

Northern Ojibwa myths often reflect the struggles and uncertainties of life in the severe Subarctic environment. The star of many of these ancient stories is the culture hero Nanabush, also known as Nanabozho, Manabozho, or Winabojo. Nanabush taught the Ojibwa the skills they needed to live on Earth. He also gave the animals their features. In this excerpt from a traditional Ojibwa tale, the hero helps his friend the porcupine, who came to Earth without any quills.

Nanabush went to the river and, before long, returned with a great armful of wet clay. He daubed the porcupine's back with the clay until he was well covered. Then the mighty magician pulled thorns from the hawthorn tree, peeled them, and stuck them in the clay. The peeled thorns turned white, and Nanabush, with his magic, turned the clay into skin. Off went the porcupine, as happy as could be—for, thanks to Nanabush, he and his descendants had gained the protection they needed against larger and swifter animals who would otherwise have harmed them.

Coyote the Sioux Trickster

A battle between the Sioux and the Blackfoot was painted on hide.

Sometimes, myths are serious tales that teach people important lessons. However, there are many myths that are great for a laugh! These funny stories are most often known as trickster tales. Almost every culture around the world tells stories about the mischief-makers. These crafty tricksters defy divine authority, the laws of nature, and accepted rules of behavior. The trickster can be both good and evil, clever and stupid, sacred and comical. However, the pranks these mischief-makers pull can cause a world of trouble, and they don't always get away with their questionable choices. At the same time, tricksters often serve as awe-inspiring creators and culture heroes.

Our stories have already introduced us to a few Native American trickster-heroes. Raven used trickery to win the chief's daughter for himself and in the process brought light to the world. Glooscap and Nanabush acted as protectors and creators in the stories shared here, but in other tales the two heroes are capable of mischief and deception.

Now it is time to meet the greatest trickster of all, Coyote. One of the best-known characters in American Indian mythology, Coyote appears in myths from nearly every culture area. This cunning rascal is responsible for introducing darkness, cold, suffering, death, and other ills to the world. He also brings fire, the buffalo, the salmon, and other great gifts. His stories are a celebration of life amid danger, laughter amid tears. For centuries they have served as a way for tribal elders to pass on the central values of their people without preaching. Coyote's antics warn us about the consequences of selfishness, greed, carelessness, dishonesty, and other undesirable qualities and actions.

This account of Coyote's adventures with his fellow trickster Iktomi was inspired by a traditional Sioux story. The mighty Sioux Nation was made up of several different tribes scattered across the Great Plains. The tribes broke up into small family bands to follow the vast herds of buffalo across the grasslands. One good buffalo hunt in the fall could provide enough meat to last a long winter. The hides, horns, and bones were used to make tepee covers, clothing, tools, weapons, and other essential items. While the Sioux were fierce hunters and warriors, they were also a deeply spiritual people. They communicated with the spirit world through dreams, visions, music, dance, and, of course, their ancient tales.

Dramatis Personae

Coyote Popular trickster and culture hero

Iktomi (ik-TOW-me) Sioux trickster who can take the form of a spider

Inyan (in-EYE-un) Mysterious rock who is the source of all things

Coyote's Coat

One day, Coyote was out walking with Iktomi, the Spider. The two friends came across Inyan, the rock. Inyan was no ordinary rock. He had the spirit of Wakan Tanka, the Great Mystery. He had existed before time, and he had created the Earth from his swirling blue blood. It took so much blood to make the seas and skies that by the time Inyan was finished, he had shrunk into a large, hard stone.

Coyote and Iktomi sat down to rest beside the big rock. The sun was shining, and they became very hot. After a while, Coyote took off the thick blanket he was wearing. "Here, Grandfather," he said to Inyan. "You must get cold without any hide or fur to cover you. I give you this fine blanket, because you have let me rest on you."

> Iktomi is a spider fairy. He wears brown deerskin leggings with long, soft fringes on either side.
>
> ~ Zitkala-Sa, Dakota Sioux

The two friends walked on. After a while, clouds covered the sun. The clouds began to sprinkle rain. The rain became a downpour. Coyote and Iktomi ran and took shelter in a cave. Iktomi was comfortable, because his big round body and long thin legs were covered with buckskins. But Coyote had only his shirt. The cold air crept over his bare neck and shoulders, and he was soon shivering.

"My friend," Coyote said through his chattering teeth, "go back and get my blanket. What does a rock need a blanket for? He doesn't feel the cold! Hurry, I'm freezing!"

So Iktomi hurried back to Inyan. "Grandfather Rock, can Coyote have his blanket back?"

"No," said the rock. "A gift is a gift. I shall keep it."

Iktomi returned and told his friend what Inyan had said. "What an ungrateful rock!" said Coyote. "That is

This Navajo basket displays a black widow spider design.

my best blanket, and he does not need it! I shall go get it myself."

So Coyote went back to Inyan. "Hey, you!" he shouted. "What do you think you're doing? Give me back my blanket."

"No," said Inyan. "A gift is a gift. I shall keep it."

Now Coyote got really angry. "You're the worst rock I've ever seen!" he shouted. "Why can't you be more generous?" Then he snatched the blanket off the rock and wrapped it around his shoulders.

Coyote ran back to the cave. Soon the rain stopped, and the winds blew away the clouds. The two friends built a fire in front of the cave and cooked up some berry soup. After they ate, they sat smoking their pipes and warming themselves in the sun.

How Salmon Came to the Klamath

Since ancient times the Klamath peoples have lived among the lakes and rivers of southern Oregon. Fish, especially salmon, have always been an important part of their diet. In this traditional Klamath tale, Coyote uses trickery to feed his belly and accidentally gives the world the gift of salmon. As always, the trickster-hero's actions teach us a valuable lesson. If the two girls had been more cautious around strangers, they would not have fallen for Coyote's scheme, and they could have kept the fish for themselves.

Many years ago, there were two Indian girls. ... These two girls ate salmon all the time. Now, no one else ever tasted salmon as there were none in the Klamath River, and no one could find out where these girls got their salmon.

One summer, Coyote was very hungry ... and he started to think of the two girls and their salmon ... So he went out in the woods and got a large piece of alder bark and cut it in the shape of a salmon. Then he rubbed deer marrow on it for color...

Coyote took out his "salmon," put it on two sticks, and set it up to cook. As it began to cook, the deer marrow dripped off, and the girls wondered where Coyote ever got a salmon. ...

Coyote took his fake fish, turned his back to the girls, and pretended to eat it. After he had finished he lay down as if to sleep and snored loudly. ...

The girls decided he was asleep, so they went down to the river, where they had the fish trap—the trap was in the river and had all the salmon in the world in it. The girls raised the top carefully and took out a salmon and went back. When they got back, Coyote was gone.

Coyote had followed the girls, and after they had gone he slipped down and raised the top to get a salmon, but he lifted the top too far, and all the salmon jumped out of the trap and swam down the Klamath River. So that is how salmon got in the Klamath River.

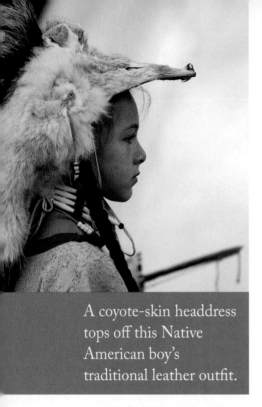

A coyote-skin headdress tops off this Native American boy's traditional leather outfit.

Ga-rum. Ga-rum.

"What's that noise?" asked Iktomi.

"What noise? I don't hear anything," Coyote answered with a lazy yawn.

Ga-rum! Ga-rum!

"I hear a rumbling noise, like thunder."

"Now I hear it, too," said Coyote. "I wonder what it can be."

GA-RUM. GA-RUM.

"Friend Coyote, I have a pretty good idea," said Iktomi.

Then they saw it. It was Inyan, rumbling and tumbling and heading straight for them!

The two friends ran as fast as they could. The rock rolled after them, closer and closer. "Friend, let us swim across the river!" cried Iktomi. "Inyan is so heavy, he will surely sink in the water."

So they jumped into the river. They swam across to the other side. But Inyan just rolled into the river and began swimming, too.

"Friend, let us hide in the woods!" cried Coyote. "That rock will never make it through the big pines."

So they ran into the forest. But Inyan just rolled after them. He knocked down all the trees in his path as if they were twigs, smashing them to splinters.

GA-RUM! GA-RUM! SMASH!

The two ran out onto the open prairie. "My friend, I have just remembered something," cried Iktomi. "I have some important business to take care of. Good-bye!" Then he rolled up his big body. He turned into a spider and scurried down a hole in the ground.

Coyote ran on. The big rock roared and rumbled at his heels. SPLAT! Inyan caught him and rolled him out flat.

The Old Man of the Blackfoot

The Blackfoot (or Blackfeet) are one of the largest tribes of the northwestern Great Plains. A popular character in their traditional tales is Na'pi, or Old Man. Old Man is a revered creator god and culture hero. Like Coyote, he can also act as a lying, cheating, bumbling trickster. This brief tale shows us the foolish side of Old Man. It also offers a mythological explanation for the way Blackfoot women gathered wild berries from thornbushes.

One day, Old Man, standing on the bank of a stream, saw in the water some reflections of berries growing on the bank. He thought them to be real berries, so he dived into the water but could find no berries. As soon as he was back upon the bank, he saw them again, so he dived one time after another, and finally tied rocks to his legs, that he might stay down longer. Then he nearly drowned. At last he was very tired, and, finding a shady place under a bush, he lay down to rest. Now, looking up, he saw the berries hanging over his head. Now he was very angry. He picked up a club and beat the berry-bushes until there was but one berry left. This is the reason why the people to this day beat berries from the bushes.

Inyan picked up the blanket from the flattened Coyote. He wrapped it around himself. "A gift is a gift," he said, and rolled back to his old place.

Soon a man came along and saw Coyote all flattened out. "What a fine rug!" he said. The man took Coyote home and put the rug in front of his fireplace.

Now, whenever Coyote dies, he has the power to bring himself back to life. This has gotten him out of many a tight spot. However, coming back to life is not easy. Because he had been rolled so flat, it took Coyote all night to huff and puff himself back into shape. In the morning, the woman of the house got up to stir the fire. When she came to the fireplace, she got a big surprise. Her husband's new rug was running away toward the prairie! Coyote ran off, cold as ever, muttering about the selfish rock who had taken his blanket away from him.

The Karuk Land of the Dead

Karuk women wove beautiful trinket and trade baskets, some with lids.

10

L ike all cultures around the world, Native Americans had strong ideas about the afterlife, or what happens to the soul when a person dies. Each Native American culture had its own ideas about what happens after death. According to some tribes, the dead lived on in a spirit world, where they continued to hunt, raise crops, and care for their homes and families in a world much like our own. However, many Native American tribes believed that the spirits of the dead could return to haunt the living. Some of these spirits might be helpful and watchful, while others could be evil or mischievous.

The Indians' differing beliefs about the afterlife were reflected in thousands of stories about the origins of death, the land of the dead, and interactions between ghosts and the living. The following story was inspired by the traditional tales of the Karuk people. The ancestral lands of the Karuk are located along the Klamath River in northwest California. Thanks to an abundance of natural resources, life was generally settled and peaceful for the people of this region. The river provided salmon, one of the most important foods in their diet. The dense forests offered deer, elk, and other game animals, as well as acorns and other plant foods. Karuk men were skilled woodworkers, producing plank houses, dugout canoes, and other objects. The women wove baskets of extraordinary strength, variety, and beauty.

Religious rituals and ceremonies were central to the lives of the Karuk and other northwest California Indians. Their ceremonies included elaborate dances designed to renew the Earth and ensure continuing good fortune. In "A Visit to the Land of the Dead," we witness one of the most sacred of these dances, the White Deerskin Dance. We also meet the mythical duck hawk Aikren. This mysterious culture hero can appear as either a bird or a man. He lives on the top of California's Sugarloaf Mountain and is the guardian spirit of the village of Katimin, center of the Karuk world. When Aikren takes pity on two grieving girls, he teaches the people of Katimin a valuable lesson about the nature of grief and life after death.

Dramatis Personae

Aikren Mythical duck hawk who is the guardian spirit of Katimin

A Journey to the Land of the Dead

Two sisters lived at the center of the world, in Katimin. They were in love with two fine young men. The men spent their days hunting and practicing the dances. Each fall, they carried the long flint blades in the White Deerskin Dance. The two maidens watched with pride as their sweethearts took part in that sacred ceremony, which gave new life and strength to the world and the people.

One day in midsummer, both young men died. In their grief, the girls thought that they would die, too. They sat by the graves of their sweethearts. The water poured from their eyes. For a whole month, all they could do was cry.

A peregrine falcon in flight

Then Aikren looked down from his nest high on Sugarloaf Mountain. He felt sorry for the grieving maidens. He flew to where they sat crying in the graveyard. He said to them, "I know where your young men have gone. Each year, I take my children to the place where people dance forever. It is a long way to travel. You must make yourselves ten dresses each. Not everyday dresses of fringed deerskin but special ones of maple bark, like those worn by the women shamans. Sleep here in the graveyard. When I am ready, my children and I will call to you."

Early the next morning, Aikren and the young duck hawks began to fly about, calling loudly. The two sisters got up and followed them. All that day the birds flew ahead and waited,

> Every morning they sat down by the graveyard, the water coming out of their eyes.
>
> ~ Imkyánva'an (Phoebe Maddox), Karuk

flew on again and waited. Up the ridge the maidens climbed after them. The mountain was brushy. The twigs and branches tore at them. By the time they stopped to sleep that night, their clothes were all worn out, and each girl changed into a new dress.

So it went, for four days and nights. On the fifth day, the maidens came upon an old woman sitting by the path. She looked as white and soft as finely worked deerskin, for she had no bones. "Greetings," said the woman. "How is it at Katimin? Is anything changed? Do they still do everything as they used to?"

The two sisters answered the woman's questions. She asked about all the old familiar places. Each time they told her, "Yes, it is just as it used to be."

At last, the woman sighed contentedly. "Those who die leave everything here," she told them. "They leave behind their clothes and their belongings and their bones, too." Then the girls saw a great heap of baskets, clothing, and other things. They passed by the pile and went on with Aikren.

Soon they came to a house. It was filled with people who were soft and white like the old woman. The maidens stood just inside the door. They watched as the people prepared to celebrate the White Deerskin Dance. They saw the dancers line up, bearing the poles that held the treasured deerskins decorated with woodpecker scalps. On each end of the line sat a dancer holding a long flint blade. Those dancers wore deerskin blankets and head feathers. Like all the dead, they were pale and boneless. But the moment the two sisters saw the young men, they recognized their sweethearts.

The dance began. As the two youths stood up, the girls tried to seize them from behind. Their hands grasped at nothing but air. The young men danced back and forth before the line of deerskins, holding out their flint blades. They kneeled again. Once more the maidens tried to put their arms around their lovers, but they could not. The men were like nothing, because they were boneless.

One of the sisters said to her sweetheart, "Come with me!"

"I cannot," the youth answered.

"Come with me!" the other sister begged her young man. But he gave her the same answer.

In sorrow, the two sisters left the house. They saw many people joining in many dances. They saw the fire pit where the women were smoking the salmon. A very old woman stood beside the fire. When the girls approached her, the woman asked, "How is it at Katimin? Do they still do everything as they used to?"

"Yes," they answered.

The old woman sighed. "Yes, all is well in the world. You must go back now. It is not yet time for you to come here. Your young men cannot go with you. They have left their bones with their bodies, and they are only shadows."

Then the old woman stripped off a small piece of backbone meat from the salmon. "When you get home, rub a tiny bit of this on the mouth of those who die," she told them.

Disease and Medicine of the Cherokee

Before the arrival of the Europeans, the Southeast was home to some of North America's most highly developed civilizations. More than one hundred different tribes inhabited this great expanse of lush forests and fertile valleys. The Cherokee lived in the Appalachian Mountain region. They were farmers, hunters, and fishermen. They built large villages of mud-plastered homes. Each village had a central council house or plaza, where religious ceremonies were held.

According to a Cherokee myth, disease and death came into the world after people failed to show the proper respect for animals. In this excerpt from that ancient tale, the animals devise their punishment, and the plants come up with a plan to save humankind from extinction.

One after another denounced Man's cruelty and injustice toward the other animals and voted in favor of his death. The Frog spoke first, saying: "We must do something to check the increase of the race, or people will become so numerous that we shall be crowded from off the earth. See how they have kicked me about because I'm ugly, as they say, until my back is covered with sores;" and here he showed the spots on his skin. ... Others followed in the same strain. ...

They began then to devise and name so many new diseases, one after another, that had not their invention at last failed them, no one of the human race would have been able to survive. ...

When the Plants, who were friendly to Man, heard what had been done by the animals, they determined to defeat the latter's evil designs. Each Tree, Shrub, and Herb, down even to the Grasses and Mosses, agreed to furnish a cure for some or one of the diseases named, and each said: "I shall appear to help Man when he calls upon me in his need." Thus came medicine; and the plants, every one of which has its use if we only knew it, furnish the remedy to counteract the evil wrought by the vengeful animals.

So, on the same day that they had arrived in the land of the dead, the two sisters started back to Katimin. Once again Aikren led the way. As they started out, he was altogether human. But as they came closer and closer to the village, he became more and more like a bird. For five days the girls traveled, wearing out a dress each day. At last they came in sight of the village. Then Aikren the duck hawk flew away to his nest on Sugarloaf.

And so the sisters came home. Before long a man died in Katimin. The girls remembered the old woman's words. They rubbed a tiny bit of the dried salmon on the man's lips. He stirred. He stretched. He lived!

The people were amazed by the heavenly salmon. For a time, everyone who died up and down the Klamath River had a bit of the salmon rubbed on him and lived again. Then the salmon meat ran out. Death returned to Katimin. But the people were not afraid. They had learned that no one ever died of grief, no matter how sad they felt for their lost loved one. And they had heard the story of the two sisters who visited the land of the dead, where the people were forever dancing.

The Myths Live On

American Indian cultures thrived across North America for tens of thousands of years. Then, in the late 1400s, white explorers arrived from Europe. The effect was devastating. The Europeans brought new diseases, ones to which the Native peoples had no natural resistance. Millions of Indians sickened and died. The white settlers also brought a new attitude toward the land, as something

Dancers participate in the Grand Entrance at a powwow.

to be owned and "tamed." As more and more Europeans immigrated to the New World, they forced America's original inhabitants to give up their lands, along with their traditional ways of life. Those who tried to resist were crushed in bloody wars and massacres. By the late 1800s, hundreds of tribes had been scattered, and some had been wiped out completely. Most of the surviving Indians had been relocated to small, isolated reservations.

Many ancient myths vanished along with the cultures that had created them. Before European contact, the Native Americans had no written languages. Their beliefs, rituals, and mythology were passed down orally, from generation to generation, by respected elders and storytellers. Around the late 1800s, European missionaries, traders, anthropologists (scientists who study human societies and cultures), and other interested people began to record the details of Indian life. Their records were far from perfect. The Europeans nearly always relied on Native American translators and storytellers, who might be reluctant to share parts of their sacred stories with outsiders. Recorders struggled to write down the Indians' long, complex narratives, which were intended for "live" tellings. They often simplified the stories they heard. Some writers edited the ancient tales to reflect their own beliefs and morals. Despite all these problems, the journals kept by non-Native recorders remain a valuable resource. In many cases they are the only published records of myths or rituals that might otherwise have been lost forever.

Despite centuries of persecution, many Native American cultures endured. In time Native peoples developed their own writing systems and began to record their traditional stories in both their own languages and English.

In recent years the peoples of a number of North American tribes have worked to recover and preserve their traditional way of life. However, this does not mean that Native Americans have frozen in time. Today many Indian boys and girls shop at malls, play video games, and surf the Internet. However, they also take part in ancient ceremonies of their tribes such as the Pueblo Corn Dance or the Northwest Coast potlatches. In schools and at home, children study age-old arts and crafts such as woodcarving, basket weaving, and pottery making. Parents and other members of the tribe keep

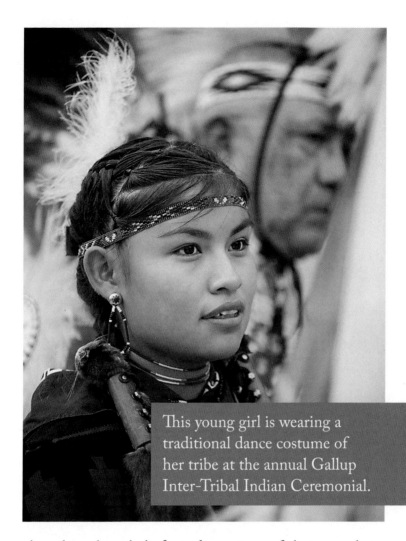

This young girl is wearing a traditional dance costume of her tribe at the annual Gallup Inter-Tribal Indian Ceremonial.

alive the values, beliefs, and practices of their people in the stories that have been passed down from their distant ancestors. They keep their heritage alive with myths. By telling these stories, proud survivors share their unique cultural heritage and make sure that the ancient tales and traditions of Native Americans live on.

GLOSSARY

Algonquian (al-GAHN-kwee-un) A large group including dozens of Native American tribes in the Northeast, Southeast, Great Plains, and other culture areas, who traditionally speak languages in the same language family, which is also known as Algonquian; a language family is a group of related languages that are all descended from the same original language.

Blackfoot A large Algonquian-speaking tribe of the northwestern Great Plains.

Cherokee An Iroquoian-speaking people who originally occupied parts of the Appalachian Mountain region of the Southeast; they call themselves the Ani-yun-wiya, or "Real People."

clan An extended family that includes people related by birth; Native American clans may also include people who are believed to be descended from the same distant ancestors.

culture heroes Mythological heroes who help humankind through their acts of courage, creation, and discovery.

earth diver An animal featured in many Native American creation stories, who dives to the bottom of the water covering the earth and brings back the mud or clay that becomes the world.

Haudenosaunee (ho-dee-no-SHOW-nee) The Iroquois peoples' name for themselves, which means "people building a longhouse."

Hopi (HO-pee) A Pueblo people of northeastern Arizona; their name for themselves is Hopitu, meaning "The Peaceful Ones."

Inuit (IH-noo-wut) Native peoples of the Arctic regions of North America and Greenland; Inuit means "The People." Outsiders often call them Eskimos, a term that most Inuit consider offensive.

Iroquois (IR-uh-kwoy) A large and powerful group of Native Americans that originally included five New York tribes (the Cayuga, Mohawk, Oneida, Onondaga, and Seneca) and later added the Tuscarora.

Karuk A tribe whose ancestral land is located on a forty-mile stretch of the Klamath River in northwest California; the Karuk call themselves Araar, or "The People."

Klamath (KLAH-muth) A group of Native tribes of the Plateau culture area, living mainly in southern Oregon.

longhouses   Large rectangular buildings made of wood and bark, built by the Iroquois and some other Native peoples.

mythology   The whole body of myths belonging to a people.

myths   Traditional stories about gods and other supernatural beings, which were developed by ancient cultures to explain the mysteries of the physical and spiritual worlds.

nation   A Native American tribe or federation of tribes.

Nez Perce   A people of the Plateau culture area, who originally traveled across parts of Idaho, Oregon, and Washington; their name for themselves is Nimi'ipuu, which means "Real People."

nomadic   Moving from place to place in search of food.

Ojibwa   (oh-JIB-way) Algonquian-speaking peoples of the north-central United States and southern Canada; also called Chippewa (by the US government) and Anishinabe (their name for themselves, meaning "The People").

Paiute   (PIE-yoot) Native peoples of the Great Basin culture area, who originally lived in parts of Utah, Arizona, Nevada, and California.

prayer sticks   Hollow reeds decorated with paint, feathers, jewels, or pollens, used to carry prayers to the spirits.

Pueblo (PWEH-blow) A group of independent Native American communities of the Southwest, including the Hopi, Zuni, Acoma, Taos, and about twenty other tribes; the word Pueblo comes from a Spanish word for "village."

Sioux (soo) A Great Plains nation made up of many different tribes belonging to three main divisions: the Lakota, Dakota, and Nakota; the Sioux peoples traditionally speak related languages belonging to the same language family, Siouan.

Tlingit (TLIN-kut) Native peoples of the Northwest Coast and islands of southeast Alaska; Tlingit means "Human Being."

tribe A group of Native Americans with a similar language and culture.

tricksters Complex mythological characters who serve as both comical mischief makers and powerful culture heroes.

Tsimshian (CHIM-she-un) Coastal peoples of southern Alaska and the Canadian province of British Columbia; Tsimshian means "People inside the Skeena River" (a river in western British Columbia).

wigwams Small dome- or cone-shaped buildings made of wooden poles, often covered with bark or woven reeds.

Zuni (ZOO-nee) A Pueblo people of New Mexico; the Zuni call themselves Ashiwi, or "The Flesh."

SOURCES OF THE MYTHS

"The Woman Who Fell from the Sky" is based mainly on the following sources:

• An Onondaga version told by John Buck, and a Mohawk version told by Seth Newhouse, collected by J. N. B. Hewitt on the Grand River Reservation, Canada, in 1889 and 1896-1897, published as "Iroquoian Cosmology" in the *Twenty-First Annual Report of the Bureau of American Ethnology, 1899-1900* (Washington, DC: Government Printing Office, 1903).

• An Oneida version told by Demus Elm (1971) and supplemented by Harvey Antone (1996), translated and edited by Floyd G. Lounsbury and Bryan Gick, published as *The Oneida Creation Story* (Lincoln, NE: University of Nebraska Press, 2000).

• Contemporary retellings by Joseph Bruchac (Abenaki descent) in *Native American Stories* (Golden, CO: Fulcrum Publishing, 1991) and by Evan T. Pritchard (Micmac descent) in *Native American Stories of the Sacred* (Woodstock, VT: Skylight Paths, 2005).

"The Corn Maidens" is based mainly on:

• A Zuni tale collected by Frank Hamilton Cushing in 1884, published in "Zuni Breadstuff," *Millstone 9*, no. 1 (1884).

- Myths compiled and edited by Katharine Berry Judson in 1912 and published in *Myths and Legends of California and the Old Southwest* (Lincoln, NE: University of Nebraska Press, 1994).

"Raven Brings the Daylight" is based mainly on:

- A Tlingit tale collected at Sitka, Alaska, by John R. Swanton in 1904 and published as "Tlingit Myths and Texts" in *Bureau of American Ethnology, Bulletin 39* (Washington, DC: Government Printing Office, 1909).

- A Tsimshian story collected by Franz Boas in 1916 and retold by Richard Erdoes and Alfonso Ortiz in *American Indian Myths and Legends* (New York: Pantheon, 1984).

- A contemporary retelling by Evan T. Pritchard in *Native American Stories of the Sacred* (Woodstock, VT: Skylight Paths, 2005).

"Glooscap Slays the Water Monster" is based mainly on:

- Passamaquoddy, Micmac, and Maliseet tales from several nineteenth-century sources, retold by Richard Erdoes and Alfonso Ortiz in *American Indian Myths and Legends* (New York: Pantheon, 1984).

- Contemporary retellings by Joseph Bruchac in Native American Stories (Golden, CO: Fulcrum Publishing, 1991) and by Evan T. Pritchard in *Native American Stories of the Sacred* (Woodstock, VT: Skylight Paths, 2005).

"Coyote and the Rock" is based mainly on:

• A retelling by Jenny Leading Cloud in White River, Rosebud Indian Reservation, South Dakota, recorded by Richard Erdoes in 1967 and published in *American Indian Myths and Legends* (New York: Pantheon, 1984).

• A contemporary retelling by Joseph Bruchac in *Native American Stories* (Golden, CO: Fulcrum Publishing, 1991).

"A Visit to the Land of the Dead" is based mainly on:

• Two Karuk myths recorded by A. L. Kroeber in the vicinity of Katimin village, northwest California, in 1902, and published as "A Karok Orpheus Myth" in *The Journal of American Folklore, vol. 59, no. 231* (Jan.-March 1946).

• A retelling by Imkyánva'an (Mrs. Phoebe Maddux), recorded by John P. Harrington and published in *Karuk Indian Myths* (Washington, DC: U.S. Government Printing Office, 1932).

Books

Brown, Joseph Epes. *Teaching Spirits: Understanding Native American Religious Traditions*. New York: Oxford University Press, 2010.

Clark, Ella E. and Margot Edmonds. *Voices of the Winds: Native American Legends*. New York: Castle Books, 2009.

Dunbar-Ortiz, Roxanne. *An Indigenous People's History of the United States*. Boston: Beacon Press, 2014.

Ferguson, Diana. *Native American Myths*. London: Collins & Brown, 2001.

Lynch, Patricia Ann. *Native American Mythology A to Z*. New York: Facts on File, 2004.

Spence, Lewis. *Native American Myths*. New York: Dover Publications, 2006.

Van Laan, Nancy. *In a Circle Long Ago: A Treasury of Native Lore from North America*. New York: Alfred A. Knopf, 1995.

Wolfson, Evelyn. *American Indian Mythology*. Berkeley Heights, NJ: Enslow, 2001.

Wood, Marion. Myths and Civilization of the Native Americans. New York: Peter Bedrick Books, 1998.

Zitkala-Ša. *American Indian Stories, Legends, and Other Writings*. New York: Penguin Classics, 2003.

Websites

Cherokee Stories
www.powersource.com/cocinc/default.html

The Cherokees of California, a nonprofit tribal organization, presents this collection of Cherokee myths and legends. Click "Stories" at the top to find a variety of myths.

Encyclopedia Mythica
www.pantheon.org/areas/mythology/americas/native_ american

This online encyclopedia contains more than six thousand entries on the myths, folktales, and legends of many different cultures. There are hundreds of articles on spirits, mythical beasts, and heroic humans.

Internet Sacred Text Archive: Native American Religions
sacred-texts.com/nam/index.htm

The Internet Sacred Text Archive is an online library of texts on religion, mythology, and related topics, which have been scanned from the original books and articles. The section on Native American religions includes translations of myths from North and South America.

Native American Lore
www.ilhawaii.net/~stony/loreindx.html

This excellent website includes retellings of more than one hundred Native American myths and legends from several different tribes. The site was once selected as a valuable Internet resource for Discovery Channel School's Discover magazine.

Native Languages of the Americas: Facts for Kids
native-languages.org/kids.htm

This easy-to-navigate site from the nonprofit educational organization Native Languages of the Americas offers authoritative information on the languages and cultures of more than one thousand American Indian tribes.

World Myths and Legends in Art
artsmia.org/world-myths/artbyculture/
nativeamerican.html

The Minneapolis Institute of Arts explores works of art inspired by mythology. Each image includes background information on the people who created the art object and the ancient stories that inspired them.

Bruchac, Joseph. *Native American Stories*. Golden, CO: Fulcrum Publishing, 1991.

Elm, Demus, and Harvey Antone. *The Oneida Creation Story*. Translated and edited by Floyd G. Lounsbury and Bryan Gick. Lincoln, NE: University of Nebraska Press, 2000.

Erdoes, Richard, and Alfonso Ortiz. *American Indian Myths and Legends*. New York: Pantheon, 1984.

Gill, Sam D., and Irene F. Sullivan. *Dictionary of Native American Mythology*. Santa Barbara, CA: ABC-CLIO, 1992.

Hardin, Terri, ed. *Legends and Lore of the American Indians*. New York: Barnes & Noble Books, 1993.

Kroeber, Karl, ed. *Native American Storytelling*. Malden, MA: Blackwell Publishing, 2004.

Lang, Julian, ed. *Ararapíkva: Creation Stories of the People*. Berkeley, CA: Heyday Books, 1994.

Lowenstein, Tom, and Piers Vitebsky. *Mother Earth, Father Sky*. Time-Life Books, 1997.

Marriott, Alice, and Carol K. Rachlin. *American Indian Mythology*. New York: Crowell, 1968.

Miller, Dorcas S. *Stars of the First People*. Boulder, CO: Pruett Publishing, 1997.

Palmer, William R. *Why the North Star Stands Still and Other Indian Legends.* Springdale, UT: Zion Natural History Association, 1973.

Pritchard, Evan T. *Native American Stories of the Sacred.* Woodstock, VT: Skylight Paths, 2005.

Rasmussen, Knud, and Edward Field. *Eskimo Songs and Stories.* New York: Delacorte, 1973.

Spence, Lewis. *Myths of the North American Indians.* New York: Gramercy, 1994.

Standing Bear, Luther, and others. *The Portable North American Indian Reader.* Edited by Frederick W. Turner III. New York: Viking Press, 1974.

Taylor, Colin F., ed. *Native American Myths and Legends.* New York: Salamander Books, 1994.

Wissler, Clark, and D. C. Duvall. *Mythology of the Blackfoot Indians.* Lincoln, NE: University of Nebraska Press, 1995.

Quoted passages in sidebars come from the following sources:

"The Orphan of the Sea," pages 34–35, from Knud Rasmussen and Edward Field, *Eskimo Songs and Stories* (New York: Delacorte, 1973).

"The Nez Perce and the Beaver," page 45, from Richard Erdoes and Alfonso Ortiz, editors, *American Indian Myths and Legends* (New York: Pantheon, 1984), based on an account in the Journal of American Folklore, published for the American Folklore Society by Houghton, Mifflin, 1890.

"The Paiute and the North Star," pages 52–53, from William R. Palmer, *Why the North Star Stands Still and Other Indian Legends* (Springdale, UT: Zion Natural History Association, 1978).

"Nanabush, The Ojibwa Hero," page 61, from Sam Snake, Chief Elijah Yellowhead, Alder York, David Simcoe, and Annie King, *The Adventures of Nanabush: Ojibway Indian Stories* (New York: Atheneum, 1970).

"How Salmon Came to the Klamath," page 67, from Evan T. Pritchard, *Native American Stories of the Sacred* (Woodstock, VT: Skylight Paths, 2005).

"The Old Man of the Blackfoot," page 69, from Clark Wissler and D. C. Duvall, *Mythology of the Blackfoot Indians* (Lincoln, NE: University of Nebraska Press, 1995).

"Disease and Medicine of the Cherokee," page 77, from James Mooney, *Myths of the Cherokee: From Nineteenth Annual Report of the Bureau of American Ethnology, 1897-98, Part I* (1900), at www.sacred-texts.com/nam/cher/motc/motc004.htm

INDEX